PLANET IN CRISIS
WILDLIFE CRISIS

This edition published in 2009 by:
The Rosen Publishing Group, Inc.
29 East 21st Street
New York, NY 10010

Copyright © 2009 David West Books

Designed and produced by
David West Books

Editor: James Pickering
Picture Research: Carlotta Cooper

Photo Credits: Abbreviations: t-top, m-middle, b-bottom, r-right,
l-left, c-center.

Front cover, tl & 29tr (Richard Jones). b & 23b (SIPA Press) - Rex Features Limited; Page3, U.S. Navy (Alphonso Braggs); 4 (Ron Giling); 5t, 24b (Adrian Arbib); 6t (Peter Weimann); 6–7, 26m (Mark Carwardine); 7bl (Fred Bavenden); 8b (Thomas Raupach); 9t (Julio Etchart); 9b (Hartmut Schwarzbach); 10b (Ray Pfortner); 10–11 (Daniel Dancer); 11l Tim Ross; 11tr, 19m, 28m (Roland Seitre); 11t (Laurent Touzeau); 12b (Aldo Brando); 14b (J.J. Alcalay); 16t (Lynn Funkhouser); 16br (B&C Alexander); 18t (Anthony Leclerc); 18tr (Cailey Ermer); 19t (Mark Edwards); 19b SoftCore Studios; 20l © Greenpeace/ Luis Liwanag; 20–21 U.S. Coast Guard (Jonathan R. Cilley); 21bm (Pierre Gleizes); 21br (Tom Walmsley); 22t U.S. Department of State; 25b NOAA; 26t F. York; 27t (John Maier); 28l U.S. Fish and Wildlife Service (Ron Garrison); 29tl (Michel Gunther); 29b (Cyril Ruoso); 29r U.S. Bureau of Land Management; 5b, 6b, 7r, 13b, 17b, 25t & b, 30 - Corbis Images. 8–9 © Greenpeace/ Grace, 21t © Greenpeace/ Beltra, 21bl © Greenpeace/ Verbelen; 26b © Greenpeace/ Kiryu; 12, 14t - USDA - SCS Photo; 12–13t © WFP/ FAO Photo; 13t - WFP/ FAO/ F. Betts; 15t (Martin Lee); 15m (Organic Picture Library); 15b (Wildtrack Media); 16bl (Michael Dunlea); 22br (SIPA Press); 22bl (WSPA); 24t (Andrew Terrill); 29l (Cavendish Press); 28r (Bachmann); 4–5, 17t, 18b, 20r, 23t - Rex Features Limited; 28br - Dover Books.

Library of Congress Cataloging-in-Publication Data

Parker, Russ, 1970-
Wildlife crisis / Russ Parker.
    p. cm. -- (Planet in crisis)
Includes bibliographical references and index.
ISBN 978-1-4358-5255-6 (library binding) -- ISBN 978-1-4358-0685-6 (pbk.) -- ISBN 978-1-4358-0691-7 (6-pack)
1. Endangered species--Juvenile literature. 2. Wildlife conservation--Juvenile literature. I. Title.
QL83.P365 2009
333.95'416--dc22

                                        2008043622

1
Printed and bound in China

First published in Great Britain by Heinemann Library, a division of Reed Educational and Professional Publishing Limited.

PLANET IN CRISIS
WILDLIFE CRISIS

Russ Parker

rosen publishing's
rosen central

New York

CONTENTS

Some wildlife adapts to humans, and even thrives. Storks usually nest in high trees, but electricity poles and chimneys do just as well.

All sea turtles are protected by wildlife laws. But it's difficult to enforce these in remote places, especially when people have an age-old tradition of catching turtles for meat, skins, and shells.

INTRODUCTION

Many people have a favorite animal, like the fierce and powerful tiger, the strong and silent gorilla, or the enduring and hardy polar bear. But all these are in danger of extinction—dying out completely. Thousands of other creatures face the same threat, from small bugs to giant whales, as well as rare trees, flowers, and other plants. The world's natural habitats shrink day by day, under attack from a huge range of human activities. To save wildlife from these dangers is a massive task. Progress is being made—but for some, it could already be too late.

"Ecotourism," like safaris on African plains, can bring in valuable funds to protect the wildlife on which it is based.

The great apes are the gorilla (shown here), chimp, and orangutan. They face many dangers from their closest cousins: ourselves.

IS ANYWHERE STILL WILD?

Some people say that we may be too late to save nature, because there are hardly any truly natural places left. Almost everywhere on our planet has been affected by people.

NOWHERE IS SAFE

Nearly every "wilderness" shows signs of human interference. Climbers conquer mountain-tops, race cars across remote deserts, and polluting chemicals find their way into frozen polar ice caps and deep oceans. And nowhere can escape the problem of climate change due to global warming.

Gazelles and lions (below) live in nature reserves that aim to recreate a wild environment. Tourists can get close enough to take photographs.

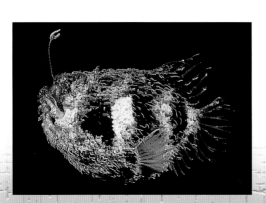

Snow leopards (opposite) live in the world's highest mountains, the Himalayas, but are still killed for fur. Even personal guards (left) cannot protect gorillas against poachers.

Hot topic

Antarctica is often called the "Last Great Wilderness." The Antarctic Treaty to protect the great southern continent came into force in 1961. But mining and petroleum companies often test it by asking for permits to explore. As we run short of fuels and minerals, will nations weaken and agree?

ECOSYSTEMS

Animals and plants of all shapes and sizes live together and depend on each other in an incredibly complex network of relationships called an ecosystem. However when people think about saving wildlife, they usually focus on large or spectacular animals like big cats and eagles. For nature to survive, the whole ecosystem and its habitat must be preserved, not just single species.

Not long ago, deep-sea anglerfish never saw the light. But now they get hauled up in huge trawl nets. These naturally scarce fish are becoming even rarer.

Emperor penguins, Antarctica

7

ENEMY NUMBER ONE

The most numerous, sizable creatures on Earth are us – humans. There are more than six billion of us, and our numbers continue to skyrocket.

NUMBERS OF ANIMALS

The most common big animals are on our farms, with 1.3 billion cattle and almost as many sheep. The most numerous, and truly wild, large animals, are probably the 15 million crabeater seals who live in southern oceans. This astonishing difference shows the numerical dominance of humans and their livestock over the wild creatures of Earth.

Tropical beaches seem inviting and peaceful. But the underwater shark nets which reduce risks to bathers—even where shark attacks are rare—take a great toll on species like the hammerhead.

WORLD POPULATION

This graph shows the increasing numbers of people worldwide since 1950, and how the rise is expected to continue. Today, three babies are born every second. The growing population will need more land to grow their food and live on, so natural areas will continue to shrink.

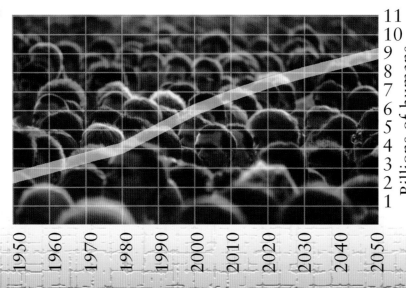

Billions of humans

11
10
9
8
7
6
5
4
3
2
1

1950 1960 1970 1980 1990 2000 2010 2020 2030 2040 2050

Being GREEN

The "dash for tourist cash" may greatly alter areas which were once relatively unspoilt. New hotels, roads, and visitor centers crowd the land. Traditional ways of life, which were in balance with nature, are being destroyed.

Chitwan, Nepal

LIFESTYLE DAMAGE

More than one billion people have comfortable homes and plenty of consumer goods, such as dishwashers, cars, and televisions. But this lifestyle damages huge tracts of nature with mines, quarries, oil rigs, cut forests, factories, and other industrial needs.

Jetting away on vacation is a welcome break for millions of travelers. But the raw materials and energy needed to build, fuel, and operate airplanes cause massive environmental damage.

DISAPPEARING HABITATS

Many different threats face various kinds, or species, of animals and plants. But one danger to the whole of wildlife far outweighs all the rest. This is habitat destruction.

BEST-KNOWN HABITAT

The world's richest wildlife thrives in tropical rainforests—or used to. Enormous areas of rainforest have been cleared to use the valuable hardwood trees for timber, and the land for crops. Rainforests may be the best-known example of habitat loss. Yet many other natural habitats disappear daily.

Tropical forests such as the Amazon are being destroyed fast, yet they are especially valuable. They could yield vital substances like new medicines.

Wetlands may look dull and empty, but their natural value is huge—as nursery areas for baby fish and other water creatures and as stopovers for migrating birds.

Red wolves prowl again.

The only major habitat which is increasing in size is the urban one. And only a few "pest" species benefit from it, like red foxes, brown rats, house mice, and cockroaches.

SAVING WILD PLACES

We can aim to save "symbols of conservation," like tigers and gorillas, in a few nature parks or reserves. But if their original homes are disappearing too, along with the animals and plants which play such important roles in their lives, eventually they will have nowhere to live in the wild. Our efforts will be wasted.

RAINFORESTS IN DANGER

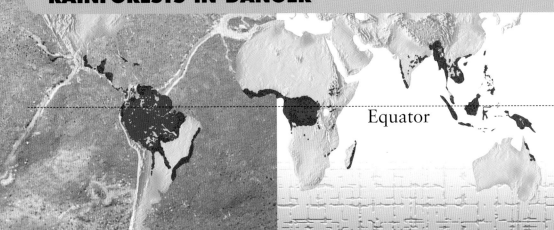

Equator

More than half of the world's rainforests were destroyed in the past century. The remainder, shown in dark green, are still being removed at a terrifying rate, with the major "hot spots" of destruction in red.

11

One type of "wilderness" is a still "wild" place unaffected by humans, where animals and plants continue to live as they did in ancient times. But "wilderness" can also mean a place with limited biodiversity, meaning a decline in the variety and number of living things.

In the 1930s, over-farming and dry conditions made areas of the United States into "dust bowls" (background). This nation was rich enough to recover, unlike many countries today.

FARMS AND FORESTS

Many such "wildernesses" are farmlands or planted forests. One crop, such as wheat or pine trees, stretches farther than the eye can see. Almost no other plants, and hardly any animals, survive in this monoculture or "one growth."

Hot topic

Even creatures on the ocean floor are not safe from hunters. Divers collect them in nets, but the biggest threats are the huge fishing boats that drag massive trawls and other nets through the sea, scraping up all forms of life. As the nets are hauled in, many creatures are unwanted and thrown back—dead.

Shellfish are at risk from divers.

DESERTIFICATION

The most common way in which habitats are degraded is desertification. Farm animals overgraze, or eat away grasses and other plants almost entirely. The plant roots die and no longer hold moisture in the soil or keep the soil particles together. In the dry season, the upper layer of soil easily blows away, or a rainstorm washes it away.

As people try to survive at the desert's edge, their cattle, sheep, goats, and camels graze and trample the soil. The soil loses its nutrients, and the animals starve.

1 Plant roots bind soil together.

2 Overgrazing kills off roots, allowing loose soil to dry out, crumble, and blow away.

CREEPING CLOSER

Every year the world's biggest desert, the Sahara, grows larger as its southern edge creeps south by two to three miles. In these dry, scrubby lands, people try to grow crops and raise livestock. But the soil is thin and poor, and droughts are common. The soil turns to dusty sand, adding to the Sahara. The same process, known as habitat degradation, is happening in many other places.

Conifer trees don't nurture much wildlife, yet more and more of these fast-growing trees are being planted to provide much of the world's softwood timber.

13

Grasslands grow where the climate is too dry for woods and forests, but too moist for scrub and desert. The problem is that "unnatural" grasslands are spreading and thriving worldwide. These grasslands are planted with farm crops and only support a small variety of wildlife.

Natural grasslands include North American prairies, South American pampas, African savannahs, and Asian steppes. Their natural grasses and plants support some spectacular animals, like the American bison. Now most of these areas are farmed and their wildlife has gone.

CEREALS FOR US

"Unnatural" grasslands are those planted with a crop like wheat, barley, rye, maize, rice, oats, sorghum, and millet. These are all cereal or "grain" plants and are members of the grass family.

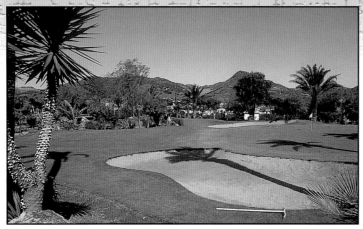

Grasses thrive on a small scale on lawns, parks, and golf courses. But most of these are mowed and weeded to keep natural variety at bay.

PAMPERED GRASS

Cereal crops cover three-quarters of the world's farmland. Farmers look after these vast monocultures (see page 12) carefully, feeding the land with fertilizers. Herbicides are used against weeds, and pesticides kill insects, so very little wildlife is able to survive.

Native grasses such as kangaroo grass and spinifex once thrived in the Australian outback. Ranchers have sown great areas with other grasses, more suitable for grazing livestock.

Hot topic

Intensive farming uses pesticides and other chemicals. In addition, GM (genetic modification) on farms is increasing, raising fears that genes may "jump" into natural species to create superpests and superweeds. Organic farms reject such methods.

Organic farm, England

Long ago, people were hunter-gatherers. They obtained all their food from the wild, by hunting animals for meat and gathering plant parts like fruits, nuts, and berries.

NEW TRADITIONS

A few people still follow these ways, like Inuit in the arctic and subarctic regions and Aboriginal peoples in Australia. Elsewhere, using modern technology, foods are taken from the wild on a huge scale. African bushmeat, for example, is a growing trade and is sold throughout the world.

A deadly trend in tropical areas is dynamite-fishing. Whole reefs are blasted, killing many fish.

In Arctic regions (above), Inuit people have hunted animals for centuries, taking only those they need and using almost all body parts for clothes and food. In Africa (left), rare species such as antelopes, gorillas, and wild pigs are killed and traded, and much is discarded.

Being GREEN

Vast curtain-like drift nets are set to catch tuna and similar fish. But dolphins also get trapped in the nets and drown. Such accidental deaths can be avoided using "dolphin-friendly" nets.

Dolphin-unfriendly

OVER-FISHING

Fast boats with harpoons almost wiped out great whales, which were finally protected in the 1980s. The same over-fishing is happening now to other sea animals, from dolphins to turtles.

DISAPPEARING FISH

Year after year, fishing fleets struggle to find more fish to catch. Because they have been so successful in the past, many places are now "fished out." In areas like the North Sea, the numbers of fish, such as cod, have collapsed.

Commercial fishing catches all kinds of animals, not just target species. Between one-tenth and one-third of catches are unintended, yet they are still injured or killed. This includes young fish who cannot then grow up to breed.

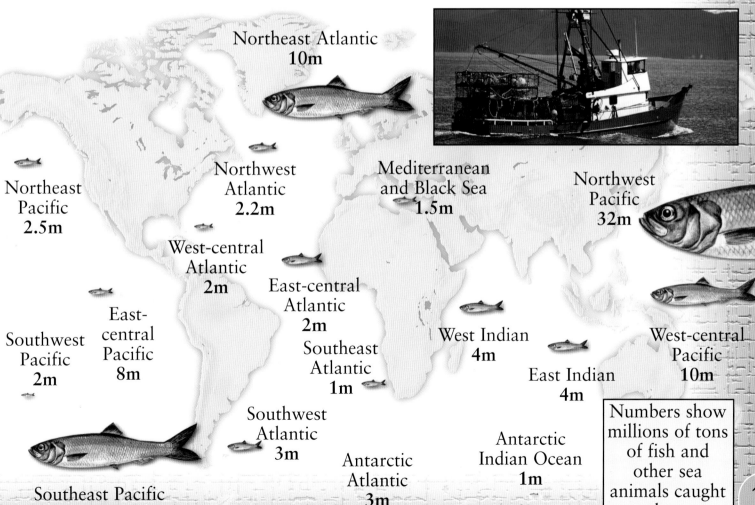

Northeast Atlantic
10m

Northeast Pacific
2.5m

Northwest Atlantic
2.2m

Mediterranean and Black Sea
1.5m

Northwest Pacific
32m

West-central Atlantic
2m

East-central Atlantic
2m

East-central Pacific
8m

Southwest Pacific
2m

Southeast Atlantic
1m

West Indian
4m

West-central Pacific
10m

East Indian
4m

Southwest Atlantic
3m

Antarctic Atlantic
3m

Antarctic Indian Ocean
1m

Southeast Pacific
15m

Numbers show millions of tons of fish and other sea animals caught each year.

17

A rabbit nibbles grass but suddenly dashes away as a red fox comes near. It seems like an age-old scene from nature—but not in Australia.

UNWANTED INTRODUCTIONS

The island continent of Australia has suffered more than most places from the ravages of introduced or alien species. These are animals and plants which have been taken from their natural or native homes to new areas. The introductions are usually carried out by people, either deliberately or accidentally.

The red squirrel was common in British mixed woodlands. Beginning about 1900, its North American gray cousin was introduced and began to take over huge areas.

UNWANTED VISITORS

Animals and plants have always spread to new regions: by natural means, such as seeds in the wind, or by creatures carried out to sea on fallen and drifting tree limbs. But people have sped up the process dramatically. Some of our introductions are deliberate, like goats as hardy farm animals. Others are "stowaways," like brown rats and house mice.

Birds easily fly to new lands.

Plant seeds arrive in bird droppings.

Insects and seeds blow on the wind.

Plants and animals drift on ocean currents.

Rabbits went to Australia with the first European colonists. By the 1880s, they had spread and destroyed vast areas of plant life.

Humans arrive with pets and pests.

One of the most widespread invaders, hiding away on cargo ships, is the brown rat. It eats many foods, including eggs. In New Zealand, it is a major threat to rare, flightless birds such as kiwis and takahes. Rats eat their eggs. Saving the birds would mean exterminating these pests.

Takahe bird, New Zealand

Goats are useful farm animals who can survive on scrubby vegetation. But this makes them very destructive, especially where local plants have no thorns or poisons to deter them.

OUT OF BALANCE

In its native home, a species is usually kept in check by predators, harsh weather, or disease. In a new environment, these natural checks could be absent. The species can multiply rapidly, upset the local ecology, and even cause its new neighbors to become extinct.

Kudzu came from East Asia. It costs the southeastern United States $500 million yearly to control its spread.

Pollution and waste affect big cities, with smog in the air, dirt in the rivers, and litter on the streets. But toxins and other pollutants spread, harming wildlife.

DEADLY SPREAD

Harmful chemicals like PCBs (polychlorinated biphenyls) are used in plastics and electrical equipment. They are released by dumping or burning. They then spread into the environment quickly, but break down slowly. These chemicals have been detected in the remotest lands. They have even been found inside polar bears!

Cleanup crews use hot water pressure hoses to scrub rocks after 58,000 gallons of marine fuel spilled into San Francisco Bay in 2007.

Highly visible oil slick pollution kills marine life, like fish and birds. But invisible chemicals take a greater toll.

Hot topic
Some campaign groups use direct action, and even risk injury, to gain publicity. Their aim is to make people more aware of the dangers to wildlife and our shared environment. These Greenpeace activists are protesting against polluting coal-fired power stations in the Philippines.

Greenpeace take action.

Dead fish litter the bank after toxic sludge escapes into a river in Spain (inset). Rivers carry pollution hundreds of miles and into lakes and oceans.

CONCENTRATING HARM

As polluting chemicals spread through air, soil, and water, they are a special danger to larger predatory animals, like birds of prey, big cats, and sharks. Plants absorb low levels of pollutants. Herbivores eat these and ingest more toxins. Predators eat the herbivores, in turn, and their pollutant levels rise higher.

BIO-AMPLIFICATION

(1) Pesticide sprays get into crops. (2) Small animals like mice eat these and gather the chemicals in their bodies. (3) The same happens as the owl eats the mice. The way that toxins become more concentrated along a food chain to harm top predators is called bio-amplification.

In richer nations, chemicals are gradually improved to lessen pollution. But older versions are sold to other countries and used without proper protection.

Beluga (white whales) have been found with high levels of toxins in their bodies. Demonstrators raise public awareness about the dumping of toxic waste in oceans (inset).

Some kinds of animals face a special threat: poaching. This is when protected creatures are illegally caught or killed. There are ways to tackle poaching, but some governments try to ignore it.

REASONS FOR POACHING

Some animals are captured alive, usually for the exotic pet trade. Colorful birds like parrots and macaws, monkeys and apes such as baby chimps and orangutans, snakes, fish, and even spiders are at risk. Other creatures are killed for body parts, such as fur, the ivory tusks of elephants and walruses, horns, antlers, teeth, bones, even blood and body fluids.

Being GREEN
International trade in animals and plants is controlled by CITES and other agreements. But illegal capture for exotic pets and "medicinal" body parts is widespread and worth $10 billion each year. Celebrities such as actor Harrison Ford campaign for an end to this cruel business.

Ford appeals on TV, 2007

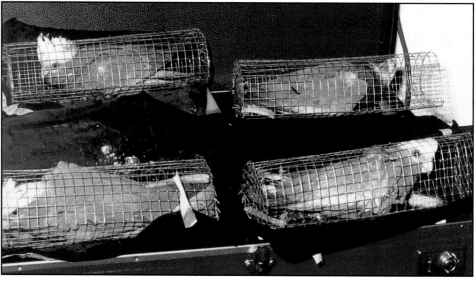

Some poachers specialize in stealing babies to be raised as pets—and often abandoned—by humans.

Live animals, like these Galah cockatoos, are smuggled in terrible conditions, and many die.

A magnificent rhino slaughtered for its horn.

SUPPLY AND DEMAND

Rare or valuable animals can be protected by guards and rangers. A long-term solution is to remove the demand. Perhaps people could do without gorilla-hand ashtrays or rhino-horn knife handles and be taught that powdered tiger-bone "medicine" has no healing value. The world agreement against poaching is the Convention on International Trade in Endangered Species (CITES).

Some African countries show their support of an ivory trade ban by burning elephant tusks, which have been seized from poachers.

PROTECTING NATURE

Around the world, thousands of wildlife parks, reserves, refuges, and sanctuaries have been set up to protect animals and plants. But only some are successful.

STRUGGLE TO SURVIVE

Many threatened species and habitats are in poor regions, where people struggle to survive. They may resent the land set aside for animals and the money spent on rangers and visitor centers, while their families go hungry. If local people are involved in running parks and using the income, there is greater chance of success.

Hot topic
Plants, as well as animals, are in danger of being taken from the wild and sold to collectors. "Cactus rustling" is big business in parts of the Americas. It's difficult to patrol the huge areas of dry scrub and protect these rare and beautiful plants, which may flower only once every 100 years.

Cacti bloom in Mexico.

Tourists shop and dine at an African nature park—but who benefits from their money?

SAVE THE TIGER - AND OTHER SPECIES

Main tiger reserves

Networks of reserves developed to protect tigers in their natural habitats also benefit other rare species, such as the Asian one-horned rhinoceros and the pygmy hog.

Tigers need their own territories.

NEED TO ROAM

Big predators like tigers and eagles need huge territories to roam, hunt, and search for mates. If they are crammed into small reserves, they may mate with related individuals and suffer from problems of genetic inbreeding. Some reserves are linked by "corridors" or pathways, for use when mating, to help the animals find unrelated partners.

SAVING HAWAIIAN MARINE LIFE

The Hawaiian marine park is home to many exotic species such as red-pencil sea urchins.

One of the world's largest nature preserves also has the longest name—Papahanaumokuakea Marine National Monument, encompassing many of the northwestern islands of Hawaii. It was established by the U.S. government in 2006 and has an area of almost 140,000 square miles.

PACIFIC OCEAN

HAWAII

Papahanaumokuakea Marine National Monument

25

Famous threatened species like gorillas and whales will only survive if we save their whole habitats. But such "headline" species also bring valuable publicity.

RAISING AWARENESS

"Headline" species are usually big, spectacular, fierce, cuddly—or all of these. They grab the news and feature in campaigns, sometimes at the expense of other threatened species. Often, however, they help to raise general awareness about saving wildlife.

Being GREEN

The quagga of southern Africa was thought to be a special type of wild horse which went extinct in 1883. In fact, studies show that it was a variety of plains zebra. The Quagga Project aims to mate selected zebras which look most like the quagga in order to revive the breed and release it into the wild.

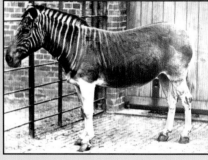

Quaggas lacked stripes on the fore and hind legs.

In the 1980s, protesters (left) helped stop the mass slaughter of great whales like the blue whale (above). However, many of their smaller cousins remain unprotected and are still being killed.

Don't go!
世界は見ている
GREENPEACE

Spix's macaw is probably now extinct in the wilds of northeast Brazil. But there are more than 120 in captivity. Saving this species depends entirely on breeding them.

All five rhino species need our protection. Four are faced with dying out. The Sumatran rhino is the smallest and hairiest rhino—and just a couple of hundred remain.

GONE BEFORE WE KNOW IT

For some animals and plants, conservation comes too late. It's estimated that there are more than 20 million species of living things, and one becomes extinct every few hours. Most of these are bugs and similar small animals in remote places. But some are bigger. The baiji (Chinese river dolphin) may be extinct—a thorough search in 2006 failed to find any at all.

When European settlers arrived in North America, vast flocks of passenger pigeons darkened the skies. Shooting, trapping, and poisoning killed off the whole species by 1914.

In 1938, a law was introduced to protect the Australian thylacine, or "Tasmanian tiger." It was too late. The last known one died in 1933.

27

Some people do not like to see animals in captivity, held in pens, or behind fences. But for some species, there is no other option, apart from dying out completely.

GAINING KNOWLEDGE

Animals in captivity cannot live exactly as they would in nature. But they can be studied by zoologists and other scientists. This builds up vital knowledge about what the animals eat, how they breed, and other information to help save them in the wild.

During the 1980s, the number of Californian condors fell to about 20. All were captured for breeding, causing huge debate at the time. Today there are over 150 in the wild, with a similar number in breeding centers. The chicks are fed by people wearing glove-puppet condor heads.

About 1,500 giant pandas are left in the wild, in southwest China. Efforts to breed them in city zoos have had mixed results. Research centers set up in their habitats are more successful.

Captive breeding helped revive the Arabian oryx, a rare antelope that went extinct in the wild by 1972. Starting in 1982, small herds raised in wildlife parks were released into the wild.

Baby apes like orangutans rely on their mothers to teach them survival skills, such as which fruits to eat.

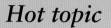

BACK TO THE WILD
Captive breeding has helped to save dozens of species from disaster. But there are problems. If the original threat to an animal was habitat loss or poaching, will there be anywhere safe to release captive-bred individuals? Some creatures like whales, elephants, and apes need long periods of learning when young—what to eat, which predators to avoid, and where to travel in their habitat. This is difficult to provide in captivity.

Animals and plants are worth saving for so many reasons: pleasure, beauty, excitement, fascination, scientific knowledge, and possible new products, like medicines from rainforests.

TOUGH CHOICES

However, it's difficult for us to decide which species should be saved. We need to think about saving nature as a whole complex system. Why not start an initiative in your school to support a species at a local zoo? You could learn more about their habitat and the dangers they face in the wild.

FOR MORE INFORMATION

Organizations

FRIENDS OF THE EARTH
1717 Massachusetts Avenue
Suite 600
Washington, DC 20036
(202) 783-7400
www.foe.org/
The largest international network of environmental groups, campaigning for the conservation of species and wild places.

International Union for the Conservation of Nature and Natural Resources (IUCN)
1630 Connecticut Avenue, NW
3rd Floor
Washington, DC 20009-1053
(202) 518-2047
Email: postmaster@iucnus.org
www.iucn.org/usa/
The IUCN monitors wildlife worldwide and helps to save threatened species.

THE NATURE CONSERVANCY
4245 North Fairfax Drive
Suite 100
Arlington, VA 22203-1606
(703) 841-5300
www.nature.org
The leading organization working around the world to protect ecologically important lands and waters for nature and people.

World Wildlife Fund (WWF)
1250 24th Street, NW
P.O. Box 97180
Washington, DC 20090-7180
(202) 293-4800
www.wwf.org/
WWF (formerly WorldWide Fund For Nature) leads international efforts to conserve nature and protect the diversity of life on Earth.

For further reading

Bow, James. *Saving Endangered Plants and Animals* (Science Solves It). New York, NY: Crabtree Publishing Company, 2008.

Johnson, Robin and Bobbie Kalman. *Endangered Penguins* (Earth's Endangered Animals). New York, NY: Crabtree Publishing Company, 2007.

Turner, Pamela S. *Gorilla Doctors: Saving Endangered Great Apes* (Scientists in the Field). Boston, MA: Houghton Mifflin Company, 2008.

Turner, Pamela S. *A Life in the Wild: George Schaller's Struggle to Save the Last Great Beasts*. New York, NY: Farrar Straus Giroux, 2008.

Pobst, Sandy. National Geographic *Investigates: Animals on the Edge: Science Races to Save Species Threatened with Extinction.* Washington, DC: National Geographic Society, 2008.

Wagner, Viqi. *Endangered Species* (Opposing Viewpoints). Farmington Hills, MI: Greenhaven Press, 2007.

Web Sites

Due to the changing nature of Internet links, Rosen Publishing has developed an online list of Web sites related to the subject of this book. This site is updated regularly. Please use this link to access the list:
http://www.rosenlinks.com/pic/wild

GLOSSARY

adapted
Having skills or features which help an animal, plant, or person to survive in a particular place, such as the thick fur of the polar bear, which keeps it warm in the Arctic.

biodiversity
A measure of the number of different kinds of living things in a particular place.

ecology
The scientific study of how a community of plants and animals live together in their surroundings.

ecosystem
A community of plants and animals in their physical environment, and especially how they live together and interact with each other.

environment
The surroundings, including soil, rocks, water, air, plants, animals, and even human-made structures.

extinct
When a species of living thing dies out completely, so there are none left, and it cannot be brought back.

habitat
A particular type of environment or surroundings, with certain kinds of plants and animals, such as a river, grassland, desert, or rainforest.

herbicide
A chemical substance designed to kill plants, especially weeds, while leaving crops unharmed.

pesticide
A substance designed to kill or disable pests such as insects, mainly on farm crops or animals.

pollutant
A substance that causes harm or damage to our surroundings, including to wildlife and to ourselves.

predators
Animals that hunt and feed on other animals.